LANDSCAPE
Fear & Love

Also by Louise Morgan Runyon:

Reborn (2004)

LANDSCAPE
Fear & Love

Poems

Louise Morgan Runyon

Louise Morgan Runyon

LANDSCAPE
Fear & Love

ISBN: 978-0-6151-6755-8

This book is dedicated to the memory of
Louise McIntosh Morgan
1910 – 2007

Table of Contents

Georgia

Acknowledgments

I would like to thank, first and foremost, those fellow writers who have given me invaluable feedback along the way: Tom Bell, Collin Kelley, Adam Cole, Marcia King, and my cousin, Michael Mack. My great thanks also to my son, Lucas Barth, for his front cover design. I thank Dan Schultz and Deborah Palmer for their help with photography, and Tom Bell, Andrew Goodman and Emily Vorder Bruegge for their computer help. I am grateful to Memye Curtis Tucker and my fellow poets at Callanwolde Fine Arts Center for their feedback; and to Several Dancers Core and The Field, where many of these poems first came into light.

I would also like to thank the family and friends who grace these poems: Brian, Lucas, Marie, Louise, Liz, Ruthy, Ana Sofia, Laurie, Perrin, Frances, Deborah, Jennie, Anastasia, and others.

My deepest gratitude goes to my aunt and fellow poet, Louise McIntosh Morgan (1910–2007), for her love and for her gift to me, as a child, of the mountains of Western North Carolina. My gratitude also goes to my uncle, John Theodore Morgan (1906–1967), who first introduced me to the world of art and whose painting graces the cover of this book.

California

Karst Country

Sandstone, karst country,
where nothing is as it seems,
where rock is sand,
where solid ground
is full of holes

An empty, possibly sinister place,
slightly desolate,
a place where crime seems possible

Old gathering place,
rounded overhangs of cliffs,
old acorn-grinding bowls,
depressions deep in granite,
bowls of different depths

A giant circle
of tiny yellow flowerets,
my child hops a dance within

I picture gatherings
where the slight desolation of today
becomes contented, pastoral,
peopled, peaceful

I see the vast meadow,
enclosed by coastal range and sandstone cliffs,
spread out under pastoral skies

late sunlight catching the green edges
of the low ridges
just as it does
today

Circles and Squares, Going West

Memphis, where already the Mississippi
is a fat snake
running through farmlands,
the shapes of all the farms irregular,
their borders formed by the tiny tributaries
of the giant

tributaries fanning out like spider veins
across the green and yellow –
no squares, no irrigation circles,
no artificial green –
here, it rains

Memphis, where the humidity was still in our hair,
where we savored the signs:
Little Rock, Tupelo, Route 66
all the historic crossroads

My friend's temporary home, in Memphis,
an extended-stay motel perched
above the Mighty Mississip,
my friend waxing glorious about the muddiness,
the history, its breadth

From the air, a little further west,
squares again, and rectangles,
the occasional trapezoids of farm,
and again in the Ozarks, and Amarillo,
the irregularity of green

Sometime later, after a summer snow-dusting
in southern Colorado
the earth dries and begins to crack –
then salt on black hills,
the desert's version of snow

Clouds form again
over the snowy Sierras,
and in the rained-on areas of California's coastal range
green growth studs the saffron hills
like hearty rosebuds

Arroyo seco

En marzo,
Arroyo seco
no es seco

In March,
the dry ravine
is not dry

but lush, green, carpeted
with wild flowers:
the blue ones, lupine and larkspur,
the gray-green sage and wavy soaproot,
the California wild lilac

a place to lie
in pastoral grass, to listen
to stillness

where Manzanita's dark red bark,
like her sister Madrone's,
is smooth as deep red waxy floor, streaked
with gray and gnarled wood

Manzanita's silver hair
is tiny strands of branches, growing upwards,
while sage-green, rounded, oval leaves
float like bracelets
on dark red arms

In March,
the dry ravine is not dry
but *arroyo seco* is everywhere

A tree bent over backwards
        till its hair touches ground
                still grows branches upwards

Dead and blackened branches
        nest in crotches
                of dead and blackened trees

The fields are strewn
with the gray and silver bones of oak skeletons,
gargantuan driftwood stallions
on their backs –

        raging stallions, hooves in air,
        nostrils flared, legs flailing –

Fields are strewn with the gray and silver bones
of oak skeletons on their backs,
their branches *cut!* through air
like tentacles,
like antlers,
waving

                Arroyo seco
                Los Padres National Forest, California

14

Little Boy Blue

Little boy blue,
Come blow your horn
Sheep's in the meadow,
Cow's in the corn

Where's that little boy s'posed to be tendin' those
    sheep?
He's offfff
in the haystack
fast asleep

His daddy loves the river bottoms –
good places to hide
his mother loves the mountain tops –
good places to be seen –
this child loves both
and the meadows
in between

This child of deep brown eyes
and speckled-trout, freckled skin,
rusty hair and red gold beard,
dressed in the colors
of sheep and fire

This child lies down
in fresh spring grass,
pulls out his flute
of cinnamon wood

and.blows
his horn

The Details of Children

Their hair –
the one's red, gold, wild, swirling
like the tall and wayward Bradford Pear
in my Georgia yard
this fall –

the other's golden, waving, rolling
like the gold and rolling hills of California
where they reside

their clothes –
the one's blue, green, gray, mirroring eyes,
only just now coming
into red – and an artist,
after all

the other's orange and rust,
the brown of eyes, the redhead's green,
with streaks of purple and rose –
clear and joyful, wild,
owning his freckles, his hair –
and a dancer,
who would have thought

their hearts:
full, tender, seeking; uncertain, unafraid
glorious, young men
coming now to own themselves,
to inherit their place
on earth

Welsh Harvest

Harvested, not made:
this salt the main taste, the zing and the comfort,
of soft large hot pretzels
bought from a cart
on cold New York days

The palpableness of it, the solid shapes
inherently iodized, unlike Morton's
not just flavor, but food
I take it on my tongue

Begotten, not made;
harvested and imported
from the land of my ancestors across the Atlantic,
my son currently carrying his Welsh middle name
to the Southern Hemisphere, where the Welsh
settled in Argentina
Halen Môn, Pur Gwyn:
sea salt, pure white

Not far from the Welsh settlements
my son hikes alone, in the wind:
never far away, in my mind,
these five small salt crystals
bring my child back,
carry me back
to my child

The Promised Land

I wanted simply to watch a kick-back movie
and only picked *The Grapes of Wrath*
because it was a fine old classic I hadn't seen in many years,
thinking of it as an historical document only,
never imagining its relevance to my life or today's world –
well, I was so wrong

It is still a fine old classic,
but there across the screen in beautiful black and white
were the same hopeful and desperate seekers,
driven from their homes and in search of the promised land,
only to find out that without
the very means to live which they were seeking,
their way was closed, the border sealed

In the 1930s it was the Okies,
in the 1960s Mexicans,
in 2006 still Mexicans
and a million other people, like me

My son lives on an organic farm in Watsonville, California
which employs Mexican farmworkers, though not so many
Do you ever talk to them, I said, you studied Spanish
No, he says, not really, only to say hello

Brian, don't you know
how many years we boycotted lettuce and grapes
        and Gallo wine,
stood out in front of the Big Star in Atlanta
trying to get the other customers to do the same
You should talk to them, Brian

He talks to them now a little bit, he says,
and during the huge recent wave of immigrant demonstrations,
and the enormous one in Watsonville, which is 90% Hispanic,
none of the Mexican farmworkers came to work that day

He says he doesn't know if John, the owner of the farm,
was at the demonstration,
but Angie and some other Anglos who work there went
That is good, I say

The golden hills of California
where my two children reside
call to me

It's been too long in Atlanta
with no family –
I think to go

What was I thinking?
Four hundred and fifty thousand dollars
was the cheapest house in Santa Cruz
on the Internet I could find

and as Woody Guthrie said in his song so long ago,
If you ain't got that do-re-mi, boys,
you better go back to beautiful Texas,
Oklahoma Georgia Kansas Tennessee

But as Ma Joad says,
home is where the heart is,
where the family is:
Route 66, California, Oklahoma,
Georgia

Reno

Reno, it was, and 1952,
where circumstances found
my mother and me, awaiting residency,
for the purpose of divorce

In 1952 in New York
a divorce was not to be had easily
but you could take the train to Reno,
stay six weeks, get a divorce, take the train back,
become a homeless single mother

Never mind that it was my father who left us
it was my mother who was left
to get the divorce

Did the train we took cross the Rockies,
stop in the little mining towns,
did it run along the green Colorado?

My mother disembarked, no doubt, in Reno
suitcase in one hand, me in the other
wearing a rumpled tailored suit, a hat
spectator pumps, perhaps

She smoked her Camels, I'm sure
surely had a drink
doubtless played the slot machines a time or two,
striking up with others soon to be divorced,
strolled me in my stroller around Reno
applied lipstick

I cried, no doubt, she may have
though the crying gene
mostly skipped her generation

How was it heading back
through the brown dust of the western hills,

across the shimmery desert?

It would have been a northern route
such as I take today
doubtless some rain, at least
by Pennsylvania

New York

New York Air

The air of New York
has a tendency to be brisk –
the city is, after all, a port, on the ocean,
the mouth of the Hudson opening to the ocean,
its geography lifting the city above its teeming streets,
over a difficult childhood,
into the air

Standing always at the bus stop
outside LaGuardia airport
I am lifted by the air, by the wind,
I am coming
not just to visit my mother, a difficult childhood,
but the geography of the place

Waiting for the city bus,
obediently, efficiently waiting, as taught to do,
I come to New York out of obligation,
not to see the buildings, but I manage
to feel the air, the bare air,
the briskness, before being confined
to overheated rooms

My reflection in the bus shelter glass,
though 35 years younger, has the same
vertical furrow in the forehead, the same
vertical ropes in the neck,
the downward turn of the mouth
hers and mine also

I ride the bus with black-leather-jacketed,
back-packed and yackety New Yorkers
I struggle off with luggage efficiently managed,
though still a struggle –
and I must stop

I walk to the corner to see the sky
and turn and look
at the brilliant, windblown, October blue
at the sprinkling of yellow leaves, even here in Manhattan
at the tiny angel, Gabriel,
gracing the tip of Riverside Church

The tiny angel Gabriel,
once visible through the dirty New York glass
of my mother's kitchen window,
now hidden from her view

I see the tiny angel,
horn raised to its lips,
giving me force, giving me hope
giving me grace, giving me power
to breathe, and go in

Coming Home, The Hardest Thing

Coming home is the hardest thing,
and the most
instructive

How much in her essence at 88
sitting at her dining room table
she reflects her Carolina forebears,
she who so unflinchingly
rejected the South

The good mother, the good Samaritan
the crusader, the tireless activist,
the railer at all things wrong

She sternly rebukes
the ebullient two-year old
who jumps down the aisle on Sunday
and makes every other single person in the church
laugh

The good mother,
did she treat me as she treats
the two-year old, her grandchildren?

I watch her stern head,
cocked and with the slightest shake
as she walks down the aisle, and wonder,
how could I ever imagine I could have a chance
with two such as she and he

I think of her sister, and brother, and among the three of them
not one really fit to have children
not to mention their parents
but have children
they did

I meet the old neighbors in the elevator and they say
Oh, you look more and more like your mother, every day

It makes it now more possible to recognize you, they say

My mother, for whom
the gin keeps the hounds at bay,
the hounds and the demons of fear and need
so that she is never, never, ever afraid –

but with one good eye and one good ear
she sees unclearly and hears unclearly
and jumps out of her skin
if you surprise her

The Subway

I stare at our reflections
in the subway window and reflect
on the once-tall, once straight-as-an-arrow
old woman, still handsome
a completely arresting, totally unusual
figure, bedecked with wrinkles
and political buttons

I stare at myself next to her:
now taller, hair darker, comparatively
straight as an arrow,
an unmistakable daughter who,
unlike her mother,
can sometimes pass for someone
quite ordinary

The two of us
irresistible to look at, lives irresistible
to scrutinize, when taken together –
and sure enough, they are looking –
How dare they stare?

I decide to catch them at their own game –
I look up and a couple is gawking
as I had imagined
I pointedly don my glasses
and fixedly turn my gaze
toward them, I succeed –
they look down,
confused

With the next invaders of privacy
I am not so lucky
they simply refuse,
lock eyes with my own

Adding insult to injury,
my mother herself stares fixedly at me
I cannot stand it
I slip gratefully, finally, into the seat in front
and refuse to turn around, pointedly ignore
her gaze at my back

But when I let my seatmate out, I see
that the seat next to my mother
is now vacant
and open

The Geology of New York

The geology of New York
I never noticed as a child, except in my bones,
except I knew I didn't like to climb as my friends did,
across the street from our apartment building,
the big gray rocks of Fort Washington
where the Battle of Harlem Heights was fought
in the revolutionary war

I noticed the cobblestones, of course, of 122nd Street,
those big gray blocks of native rock, long since paved,
hardly ever saw the Hudson, just blocks away,
never knew the Hudson River Valley.
Never climbed on the gray crags of the Palisades
across the Hudson, just heard of them,
thought of them only as
Palisades Amusement Park

The grand architecture of Manhattan,
reflecting the sheer fact of available building material,
the geology of New York,
the big gray rocks everywhere
in all the parks

But now, though still I hardly know it, except in my bones,
the gneiss and the schist of the rocks in the parks
the foundations of the great buildings
the heavy curbstones, the Palisades and rock walls
the great breadth of the Hudson
impress themselves upon me

I know so little of it, but get a sense, a glimmer,
of the beauty and the grandeur of the natural world of it,
so covered over by Times Square lights,
smoke-ring-blowing billboards, cars
jutting out of buildings,
while underneath –

so far from the land I *really* know
(its beauty always pointed out) –

so far from the blue mountains of North Carolina –

those gentle mountains of my ancestral home,
sleeping giants covered with green army blankets,
great gentle beasts you could nestle down in,
or whom you could straddle and ride –

so far from those blue mountains,
underneath "New York"
is a wild and rugged island, a majestic river valley
made from solid bedrock, gray gigantic rock,
the river cutting through it
in its rush to the sea

Skating Rinks, and Deer

It was the trees that pulled me onto campus, in the dusk,
a detour on my walk,
those smallish bare New York trees
shrink-wrapped in tiny Christmas lights
strands wrapped less than two inches apart
around each of 50 trunks, hundreds of bare limbs

Sick, heavy with cold, I trundled,
hands pressed against my heart,
my chest creaking like the iron bands
wrapped around a barrel

It is astonishing the depths of anger that can be found,
a hell-fired anger so profound
as to split an iron freighter in two,
an iceberg submerged in the depths;
and sometimes a person must sit
on a park bench sideways,
winter rain coming down into her face,
head hanging low, not caring

To my left, on the grassy stretches
where Columbia boys played frisbee in the 60s,
my eye catches an expanse of white
spread out over the grass – what on earth?
Could that be ice, a skating rink?
Water poured by the university to give the children a rink?

Painted black chain link fence surrounds the grassy stretches,
the gates are locked – there are no skaters.
I see that it is not ice, but canvas of some sort
stretched out across the grass, pulled tight

Oh – and I thought that perhaps it was like the deers,
the story that my friend tells
of how one Christmas eve at three in the morning
her daughter's missing luggage finally arrived in Baltimore,

my friend cranky, furious, groggy,
the Ethiopian UPS man on his cell phone,
trying to get his bearings:
I'm at the corner of Alumina and Alumina, he said,
and it was snowing, my friend eventually realizing
he was standing at Alumni Hall,
the name written on intersecting walls,
when suddenly the Ethiopian man said,
Oh! Oh! Deers!

Deer, in the snow, on another college campus
at 3 a.m. on Christmas eve,
10,000 miles from Ethiopia; heart broke through,
my friend laughed, and everyone
was redeemed

But there was no ice here, at Columbia, no skating rink –
just stretched canvas, and me
for all the world a vagrant on a park bench

only – a little farther on –
at the top of the shrink-wrapped, twinkling, detour-causing
    branches
of one of the bare trees

a large nest, dark against the sky
baby birds in it, visible, chirping
why born now, who knows?
they normally are so camouflaged
by green

Billions of Daffodils / Blind

Flowers did not grow
in New York City in the 50s,
but now there are a billion daffodils
blooming in New York

I walk slowly through the park,
the day is beautiful but I am unable to bear
any of the passing people
I walk and cry and sit and cry
I talk out loud to myself, I have no tissues
the daffodils abound, my mother's favorite flower

My mother, who hated her own mother –
ah, but she had siblings
who cared for their mother at the end
my mother wore dark glasses
the day her mother died

My mother doesn't believe in doors
and has no guest rooms in her ten-room flat
My cousin, whom I have never met before,
sleeps without his clothes and is attractive

I must share sleeping space with this cousin,
my suitcase by his head and his by mine,
my mother thinks nothing of it
he walks to the bathroom, pink towel around his hips
Let me have that towel
my mother says, cutely, grabbing
my mother, who is blind

I walk slowly through the park
The day is beautiful and I am unable to bear
any of the passing people
I put on my New York blinders and ice
every single person that I pass: there are so many

The only ones, after several hours, it doesn't hurt to look at
are the 8- to 10-year old boys
and some of the women who are friends

Heritage

My mother is the daughter of an orphan
whose mother died and whose father,
in the custom of the times,
gave her up to the orphanage,
being unable to care
for her

My mother
is the daughter
of an orphan,
my grandmother was an orphan

This may explain how she held me
in the sepia-toned black and whites,
held down with silver corners:

"Weezie at 3 weeks, with Gin-Gin"
my grandmother, holding me out like a prize
a prize held out, a thing to be admired
not a being to be held
in close, or nurtured

In another photo I am two,
my own proud mother gazing
off into the horizon, head back,
proud carriage, unfolded,
with me in the crook of her arm
in boy's hand-me-downs
raggedy Floppy under my arm
cowlick up and eyes cast down
just scratching
my ear

Cornbread & Lace

My grandmother's hand on a small torn envelope:
For Weezie
Below, in brown ink, a note to my mother:
Please let me know at once about the check
so I will know whether to look for a hat

this from the days when money was tighter
and people wore hats

Inside the envelope, marked with my name: lace
of the tiniest, most delicate kind
with a note from my mother, saying
It's possible the lace was hand-crocheted
by one of your great-great-grandmothers

My mother always said that Gin-Gin,
the grandmother whom I named,
never did anything, couldn't do anything
except be neurotic and complain,
while my mother led struggles
and did important things

But Gin-Gin sewed clothes and made at least two quilts
and recognized the importance
of inherited lace

And in a small scene that often comes to me
of visiting a sometime friend of my mother's,
I am sitting on the floor of the friend's living room
while they talk, making doll clothes from scraps

It comes to me that it was actually my mother
who taught me how to sew,
and nothing else means as much as this fact

In between the jewels and crowns,
the notoriety and the fame,

is also the smell of buttermilk, tangy,
and the blotted paper, folded and refolded –

my mother's recipe for buttermilk cornbread
come down through generations,
requested by my own child
over the internet: please send

Upstate

The Hudson River Valley was unknown to me,
growing up in New York City in the 50s
I was well-schooled in the cartoon map,
the poster-sized *New Yorker* cover
still gracing my mother's hallway wall,
the Steinberg cartoon in black ink and pastel shades,
Manhattan occupying nine-tenths
of the United States

But I have now twice
made the train ride up to my cousin's home
along the wide and beautiful river,
and now I have gone
all the way to Rhinebeck –
the river still wide when you get there –
and discovered

the sunlight that illuminates the maples there
just before sundown;
illuminates the maples, the maples only,
glowing like orange crowns
against the steel-gray clouds that hang over the pale lake,
one group catching the light now,
then another

Easter Sunday

Fourteen years old I was
and I thought to tell Bencie Moll,
with whom I sometimes did things,
my father died this weekend, I said

Bencie turned around in her seat in homeroom
with her dry, pale brown hair,
looked me in the eyes with her own gray ones, and said
I don't believe you,
turned quickly back

My father died on Easter Sunday
I never knew him

My uncle and aunt, as they did so often,
had driven to New York
we had just eaten Easter dinner,
lamb and mint and new potatoes,
were sitting on the couch
when the phone rang

My mother came back and said that it was my father,
that my father had just died
his last wife called because he always said
that Marie would know what to do

Marie did; she took a cab
down to the West Village apartment in the rain
to see the husband not seen in years
and called an ambulance

Forty-one years later,
having traveled to New York for Easter,
I am yelling at my mother who,
on the elevated platform, freezing,
adamantly refuses the suggestion
of hat, gloves

Freeze, I say
ninety-one years old be damned,
do what you want

She shivers, almost shakes,
a 25-minute wait for the train,
one just missed, my fault we missed it
freeze if you please, I say
she who's had pneumonia
many times

At the end of the long cold wait and the train ride north
we walk into my cousin's home,
into open arms and reasonableness,
different colored roses blooming in pots,
the warm smell of lamb

Church

With my vision blurred the Easter lilies
and red tulips on the altar
could be the poinsettias and chrysanthemums of Christmas
on this cold Easter, cold as Christmas

The toothless, homeless man in the choir,
tall and gracious in dark-red robes and gray dreadlocks,
lisps robustly into song,
bringing life into the dying boredom
of the music of the Episcopal church

A.D. 1828
is carved into a white stone plaque
on the inside brick wall,
nothing this old is in Atlanta
a 97-year old parishioner wears a button:
1/20/09

I look in vain for the indelible inscription,
"Gift of Miss Dorothea Todd," in the prayer book
that lady long dead, tall and elderly
with natural white-blond hair,
brown oxfords and watery, clear green eyes,
the donor of many books

Jesus, *Señor Jesus:*
his resurrection would stun
even the most jaded New Yorker,
says the priest in Spanish and English
The priest, another railer at all things wrong,
head thrust forward in front of his heart,
strains the voice in his throat;
my mother beside me
strains to hear

Jesus floats, as he did when I was a child,
in blue and white robes
on the round, gold-ringed canvas behind the altar
the ancient, robust organ resounds

Thin, old, dark red carpet in the pews intersects
with new, bright red carpet running down the aisle
the original brick interior, the old dark wood
survive

Corner of the Plane

My old, long-single mother
must have dance partners
and has them
while I, unescorted, manage one,
aside from her
She looks magnificent on the dance floor
I have never seen my mother
dance before

I give, I snap, once finally in my seat,
my mother safely stowed across the aisle,
bouquet of Queen Anne's Lace clutched in hand
along with her drivers' license
who knows if she will *ever*
stow it away, WHO CARES?
I want to shout
to the whole plane

I dissolve, notwithstanding the man
sitting one inch from me
or the flight attendant
whose jumpseat faces mine

I turn my face into the small window and weep
blessedly, finally,
the Vermont wedding and the almost
unbearable burden of escorting my mother there
now behind

She sees not, she hears not,
she could if she wanted to:
I know it

The ridiculous fears, the incredible demands
the cuteness, the necessity for spotlight
now on one-hour hold

The tiny propeller plane rises above Vermont,
its crimson trees and oh, the exquisiteness
of the shimmering mirror of Lake Champlain,
looking like a lake in China

My heart lifts with the beauty of it,
dissolves again as we rush upward into cloud
where we are nothing but fog, a tiny window
and a single black propeller, whirring

The stewardess passes over
a box of Kleenex
via the man

My heart calms as we rise
over the lavish clouds and blue horizon,
falters briefly as I miss the bride
who offered an outpost of love and support
in my mother's home

A halo now surrounds the propeller
as its mere three blades
catch the golden sun

We fly over the obelisks of Manhattan
with no possibility of crashing into them,
though I can envision falling onto their needle points –
Ground Zero is the empty space below,
clouds cast a pall
over certain neighborhoods
in Queens

City of my birth, magnificent to fly over
though it never feels like home

Just the two of us now and no one else,
ending, unbearably, as we started:
alone

My face crumples, finally,
as I watch my tiny little mother,
once so grand of posture and of bone,
tottering up her steps, wildly insisting
on holding the door open for me
she lives so far away from me,
alone

Sugar and Iron

Molasses, or *mislasses*, as my younger child used to say
a straight, pungent teaspoonful
brought me to my father
not from known memory but from stories
my mother used to tell
of how he insisted that a teaspoonful be poured
into every baby bottle of non-mother's milk –
for the iron, I think

For the iron! For the irony –
perhaps, as a baby, I needed iron – I wouldn't have him
But for the sugar – which perhaps I needed too,
lacking the sweetness of my mother's milk

In any case he was a 50s health nut, and insisted
and my mother says that all the other mothers on the drive
where she pushed me in my old-fashioned black baby carriage,
huge bonnet surrounding my fat baby face,
all the other mothers on the drive
always thought she was giving her baby
chocolate milk

Chocolate milk, which I grew up drinking,
something poisoning the taste of regular milk for me
as the dropping and the breaking of her baby bottle,
among other things, did for my mother

Three weeks after Christmas I can drink
neither chocolate milk nor *mislasses*,
tests having revealed my blood sugar slightly high

But at Christmas
I drank the straight and pungent teaspoonful
of blackstrap molasses,
the burnt taste smelling of the very inside of the earth,
and got a dose of my father's iron
a gift from my father
to me

North Carolina

The Sisters: Louise and Marie

She has confusion – I call her when I can
It is OK, though it is not enough,
I will want and need more
My mother's greatest gift to me, perhaps,
this sister who so plagued her

This sister who laughed with me,
we giggled like schoolgirls who couldn't help it,
pulling army blankets on army cots up to our chins
as we searched for shooting stars,
camped out on the sleeping porch, tin,
that burned my feet so
when I hung the wash out, summers

Summers, my mother sent me to her sister, south –
summers – my mother's time
of passion?

And I recall Mona Offenbaum
from my New York neighborhood,
tall, stylish, auburn-haired,
auburn hair piled high in a bun,
high heels and straight, shapely skirt,
standing on the corner
every school night it seemed, waiting
what was she waiting for and for whom,
and why was it that she didn't wait at home?
she had a daughter around my age

And what about those of us
who don't wear our auburn hair piled high,
what do we lose?
and what do we find, I wonder

I wonder as I care
for my mother's sister and my mother,
even though I am not there –

the passion and the shooting stars
now so many years ago

Perhaps we find our hearts, our hearts,
perhaps we find our souls –
if not our hope, our hope,
if not our passion, our passion

Piecing It Together

On the phone she speaks of balance
and did I agree
that that was where the truth lay,
and let the little children
come unto me

She opens her eyes when I come there,
when I speak her name, and responds;
otherwise she is deeply engaged, eyes closed
deeply engaged in the business
of figuring something out

In the business
of figuring something out,
grasping at delicate threads,
piecing together what she can
with bent fingers

It grieves me so, she says,
that my mind is gone

Her eyes are closed
as I stroke her arms and legs and back and hands
the stroking part of her dream which she accepts, smiling
it becoming the background for the piecing together
and let the little children
come unto me, she says

She allows herself to be read to in the sun
Dr. Seuss, and laughs, and takes it all in
in, to that deep place far inside,
that place that she looks out from

As soon as we get inside she closes her eyes again,
and opens them only when spoken to

She agrees, finally, to a drive –

I cannot imagine –
will I drive through the mountains
with a sleeping woman by my side?

We get lost, I don't quite know the way
she complains a little (though nowhere near as much
as before) that it's getting late
her eyes stay open
the two whole hours

Two whole hours we drive
through glorious spring mountains
alongside full creeks almost level with their banks
and broad shallow rivers
she can see them all

She looks out and takes it all in,
looks out from that deep place, and brings it all in,
and although she ate only ten noodles for lunch,
one strawberry and two bites of an egg
but all her dessert,
she allows as how she could use
an ice cream cone,
vanilla

Aunt Louise, Eating

The first thing and the last, of interest:
the inside of her own mouth

A mouth full of crooked teeth, all her own
(some of mine are crooked too, but not so many),
she has always been fastidious about her teeth
now she takes her time, eating

A meal can take two whole hours:
strawberries clear the mouth easy and fast
breaded chicken and banana bread
take forever for each bite

Red strawberries on a red plastic plate –
she wears a red dress and red jacket, my sweatshirt is red –
there is barbeque sauce
for the chicken

She dips a strawberry into mustard,
it seems to go down just fine
she calls the berries by name, says the words "banana bread" –
otherwise, volunteers little

The banana bread she wants to dip
into the barbeque sauce, and seems to like it
on the meal goes, slowly, sauce on everything
taking her good sweet time to chew,
spitting out anything
she doesn't like

slim

slim, to basics: my aunt
long, slim, bare legs
under the afghan,
the nurse's assistants look up
in the half-light –
my son and I back out,
so she can be changed

my house holds her house
so many years, already:
the wormy chestnut corner cabinet
less cluttered, but still housing
pewter made by my grandfather,
a purple-flowered white china platter
owned by my grandmother,
the hand-enameled bowls and plate
made by her, by my aunt –
what does craft mean, in our family

is it the mechanical device inside her
that keeps her alive? we wonder
she sleeps on, living, sleeping mostly –
still, she can play the harmonica

the indigo-dyed handwoven coverlet of wool and cotton
that hangs in my doorway,
made in the 30s by an unknown weaver
the name *Penland* still conjures magic
on all of our lips

how I feel after I cross the state line, from Georgia:
Welcome to North Carolina
Motorcycles Burn Headlights
this sign at all North Carolina state lines –
the road rides differently,
the vegetation is more green,
my breath comes easier and my heart lifts –

North Carolina, her beloved state
my heart, my ancestral home

miracle

her breath comes hard and fast and slow
her rock-strong heart beats
as always

her eyes open,
tiny slits but I can see
herself in there, her knowing
she lies as placed,
only her jaw moves once
or twice

all her energy goes to breath
she breathes and breathes and breathes, loudly
here and there, she pauses
we hold our breaths
she breathes again

at night her eyes shut closely tight
she has business
to attend to

in the morning
the miracle happens, so quietly
a miracle
that this rock-strong heart
could stop

Somehow, after the death

somehow, after the death
of my aunt at ninety-seven
things begin, perhaps,
to fall in place

a week I do not go out
in public and then
the friendship of friends is sweeter
and richer than I have known

I ease and set things right
with my aunt's things
my own self comes clear

I flash a smile that has brilliance
I had not remembered

perhaps
as my friend says is true in Africa
life is sweeter, stronger, richer
in the presence of more constant death

Georgia

Rock Bottom Fear

When I stepped off the edge of the cliff
on the first day of the new millennium
I knew that my heart would keep beating
I didn't know how
but I knew that it would

But when the dog trainer
gave me the leash the other day
I had to say
I had done all I could for then,
I had had enough,
the teeth and the fear
overcame me

I put my dog out,
came back and sat on a chair
kept on sliding down to the floor
kept getting back up to sit on the chair
kept sliding back down
trying to find ground

From where comes this fear,
this incessant, rock bottom fear?

Bred in the den of the mother,
spawned by departure of the father,
crystallized by the dresser in front of the door,
the butcher knife behind?
Stepping off that other cliff,
for which there was no answer?

Or did it come from Boy,
the yellow Spitz,
who bit?

At the end of yesterday
I found my pillow finally,

like a sled dog digging an ice hole
for comforting sleep
I cradled a second pillow in my arms,
felt enfolded completely, slept so soundly

I awoke only with the tiredness
of having been on a journey
and decided to look at fear
in profile only, for the moment,
sideways,
just as a dog-whisperer
approaches a dog

Above The Tree Line

There is something about
the way the wind blows and it gets cold
as you walk up the walk-up trail
of low-altitude Stone Mountain

There is something about the last one-third
where the gradual grade of granite and forest
gives way to granite alone
rising almost
straight up

There is something about the rush of air
in that last one-third
that makes crime seem impossible,
that makes you feel confident
to hike alone
as a woman

There is something, too,
about performing onstage, naked,
in a darkened theatre, under light,
that fills you with power,
a power you must respect, even
the audience
doesn't have it

There is something
about welcoming a stranger
into your studio
who trusts you enough to lie down on your table
and allows you to move the shoulder
that guards his heart
and to hold in your hands
his precious head

Do you mean to say
that no crimes have ever been committed

past the 2,000-foot mark
on the 3,000-foot granite outcropping
known as Stone Mountain,
Georgia?

I feel sure that they have

But

There is something
that has something to do
with faith
and hope
and the need for all humans
to stand without fear

and without fear
                        we stand

The Ducks Come Snaking

Just an oblong shape
but I knew it was a heron, front-on
a sudden turn and it quadrupled, quintupled,
not only long beak but long neck
elongating toward the water,
a long, long, big bird

Next I saw twin geese,
identical goose and gander,
unseen legs paddling their still bodies
in tandem through the water

Then I heard a rustle, the soft paddle
of two ducks come snaking through the reeds,
their comfortable, egg-shaped bodies different,
one variegated, a camouflaging white and brown,
the other signal bright, an iridescent green,
their comforting clucking and soft paddling
giving small, partial soothing
to my distressed heart

a small silver fish leaps
in the brown water

The heron deliberately, methodically
plucks and places its long legs and feet
in and out of the water

The geese honk and take off to the southeast,
flushing the water below them
until their silhouettes and honking
both are gone

The heron extends its long legs behind itself,
spreads its huge span and follows
but stops, still in sight
on the far side of the pond

I extend *my* long leg
from the low bench to the high rung
of the lifeguard chair, and find my perch

I can still see the male duck through the reeds
green head, black bead eye
the yellowish bill, its nostrils

the bellows of my lungs slowly fill
the ducks paddle
through the brown reeds

Circle In The Sky

There are always birds on the wires
that string across Lawrenceville Highway
at North Druid Hills Road, I often notice
Today they collect
in a multitude on a single wire
strung over the Publix parking lot,
the wire thick with them

The profusion of birds lifts off from the wire
in staggered, sequential groups
till eventually they form a swarm,
a swirl, above the highway,
forming and re-forming
to the classical music on my radio
like so much DNA
swirling

As the symphony swells, the birds
group and scatter,
separate to form a circle in the sky,
a great lush folk circle dance,
briefly suspended,
of pigeons

In quicksilver, split-second timing
the birds make and re-make
complicated, intricate
arrangements and re-arrangements
as the violins rapidly rise and fall,
the birds' wide circle opening out
a place wide
in me

Plug In My Heart

A little bit like the stem of an apple
which you twist off as you say the alphabet
and which finally comes off on the first letter
of your lover's first name
and is then stuck into the apple's flesh
and pulled out,
this plug in my heart

Or like the stem of a pumpkin in fall,
which you can grab
by hand

This plug in my heart,
this stop-gap measure,
is taken in hand by a fist
and pulled out, leaving a hole

so that now,
things can get out
and things can get in

The Jewel and the Curl

In creating dance, they found:

the tiny jewel
that is inside each one of us, he said
residing inside layers and layers
of socialization,
that tiny jewel
                  still sparkling

and his face,
so open and rare,
the red-gold hair receded so
that only a curl
stuck out the top of his head

he looked
like a baby, she said –
a curl on the top of its head –

that rare,
              that open

Tango Rain

To dance tango,
you must listen to the heart of a woman.
— Cacho Dante, *milonguero de*
Buenos Aires

Above the shoulder of my partner
I watch the lightning and the downpour
through the tall arched window
of the church

I have a sense of sailing,
of oneness, and of sailing

Lights outside the church
illuminate the rain,
making it electric and sizzling white,
rain like sparklers
against the blackness of the night

Late that night I watch the rain still falling,
through my open window now,
the tiny Christmas lights from the inside of the church
and the silver rain, electric, from without
dancing, intertwined, in my mind

Two nights later
the rain comes again,
this time to tango class,
falling hard and straight
and solidly down

Two men from Argentina,
one sweet and young, the other not so young,
offer their cheeks to me
for a kiss

I am touched by their sweetness,
cannot locate the walls and barriers

I have come to expect here,
among men of my own country,
cannot find the lines of demarcation
delineating young men from older women,
midlife women from midlife men,
can only feel the friendliness and the sweetness,
no other messages
mixed in

Late that night I lie on my bed
and the rain comes down again
solidly, solidly,
straight, straight down

The music of the tango
begins to take root in my brain,
for the first time I hear it
when it is not here

I open my blinds and feel myself as earth,
being met without detour
by the freshness, and the sweetness
of the welcome, needed rain

Break

Flat as a tablecloth, slightly rumpled
is how it's been
this winter

and now –
I need a break

I put my dog out, I bring my dog in
I avoid my taxes, I go shopping
nothing helps

the tulip bulbs I slaved over
in the dying light last fall
push out and bloom,
but I am still underground

I push against the understory of the earth
with both fists and both feet
like a dog digging a hole in reverse
but the undercrust is thick,
I cannot get through

I've had the necessary frost but cannot find
the sunlight or the nitrogen,
I am not being fed

Life is as big and imperfect, impetuous and insistent in me
as in any bulb
Like a dog, I need to roll and romp,
tear off my clothes,
streak through the woods,
find the gentleness and the fear,
the raw, the soft space, the primitive place,
the risk

I need to break
into the unknown, into hotness,

feel the cold air
on my skin·

Thinking About the Irish

I am thinking about the Irish
as I bend low in the January cold
in Georgia,
fitting the carefully cut potato pieces
into the earth

I am thinking about the Irish
and the thoughts are chilling,
of bare bones farming
and famine

My thoughts are bleak
as I squat in the January wind,
go searching for leaves in the freezing rain

I pause to remember why I do this
I think past bleakness and January despair
and remember
that these pieces of potato are umbilical cords
binding us to earth

and so it is later with the picking
of the lettuce and the beans,
the time-consuming washing and the cutting,
the long preparation of the big
spring or summer salad,
the time it takes
to chew

and so with the periodic harvesting of mint,
the drying, the meticulous separation
of leaves from stem,
the drinking
of tea

and I know why I do this,
that it all starts
now

Coming Alive

Coming alive,
coming alive at dusk,
this pond

When I arrive many cars are parked
Is this a convention I ask
and am informed

that tonight the woodcock
will have its mating display,
will soar across the sky between 6:15 and 6:40 p.m.
plump, chicken-sized birds
going "peeeeeee, peeeeeee"

How do the ornithologists communicate –
do e-mails announce,
the woodcock mated in Dahlonega
on Saturday, catch them in Decatur
on Sunday?

The woods fill with silent flashlight-bearers,
some hidden behind a bamboo blind,
each with their own
binoculars

Alone among the birders
I sport no binocs,
but perch on my favorite railing,
the highest point above the pond

the pond still, silent –
no ripple, no sound
no mating call

Sunset begins, the sky to the south
turns an orange sherbet color,
filling the bowl of the basket of the trees

the dark pond between the grasses
reflects pale pink, gray
the sky behind me is layered in pink, blue,
streaked with the white
of jet stream

out of the corner of my eye comes a heron,
gray and regal,
its shoulders elegant in flight,
winging its way across the vastness of the pond

There is a ripple in the water,
I stand on my rail to see

A chittering begins,
like little ducks or constant frogs,
thin peeps interspersing

we wait to see

New Mexico Blue

Above the scarlet geranium,
above the huge golden dome of the St. John's Wort
and the stand of tall outrageous poppies in red, white, lavender
    and pink,
is the sky today
impossibly blue, as they say

Impossibly blue for Georgia
for as anyone knows
who's flown coast to coast many times
and always looked out the window,
somewhere over Colorado the clouds clear and you can see,
and on the way back east, after Colorado, you cannot

What you can see on the way out west
is brown and black and white,
white peaks and blue lakes, desert and no man's land,
precious little green

If you drive
your hair bushes out with the humidity
and somewhere after Memphis
goes to stringy like a Texas tie

Faces wrinkle on people in the desert
and you become one,
with stringy hair, wrinkles, face turned brown

Ah, but the sky – the sky is that sky-blue
so rarely seen over lush summer Georgia:
infusion of cobalt, New Mexico blue

Window

The window of my yard, always changing,
that patch of sky framed by trees and fence and roof,
the window always opening to a different view

Today that patch is sky-blue,
reflecting the floating globes of my sky-blue hydrangeas,
the first new pinkish-purple cones of the butterfly bush
picking up the floating spheres of the lone, single pink
     hydrangea,
my white hydrangeas mirroring
the cotton clouds

Like the buttercup-yellow of the blossom-covered St. John's
     Wort,
huge and rounded behind the fence,
the light, my eyes, my vision
heightened, clarified

A tiny rose, perfect and red, rises from the other side
as the outrageous, fantastic, spiked and brilliant crimson plume
     of a single bergamot
pushes through the wooden slats, below

In front of, around, above, beyond: green, blue
my heart no longer bottled
but just a little breathless,
waiting

Fall, Change

On the cul-de-sac
where my neighbor Lynn and I sat on the curb
watching our children on their bikes
learn how to ride

there's a for sale sign in Sophia's yard,
the stuff Christina left when she moved is on the curb,
Jan's driveway is empty, she is in Florida this week,
a squirrel lies dead in the street

Lynn has long since moved
our children are now all grown

The fire hydrant in my yard
has just been painted a brilliant yellow
without my knowledge,
bringing out the riot of color
of the swamp sunflowers I planted
last fall

I pass PJ's and remember
that her dog, Dora, whom I loved,
has recently been put to sleep

In my garden
fresh new zinnias in October,
planted in August,
which the hardware store man said
should not be planted then –
fat, red zinnias and greenish-white ones,
along with greenish-white butterflies,
these mixed in with cosmos, orange

For dinner, eaten outside,
green and oily pesto, on pasta,
made from the riotous abundance of basil
in my garden this summer

The evening star shines in the pale dusk
by the time I get where I'm going, its background
is a deepening blue

Miracle

I have a teacher who is seventy-six,
when I saw her after some time
I asked about her boyfriend, Manny.

Oh, Manny, she said, he is fine.
Manny will meet me in Switzerland.
Manny, my miracle.
Six years now, you know?
I met him
when I was seventy.

Yeah, well,
I'm still waiting for my miracle,
I say.

Oh you,
you, you, you –
you will find your miracle,
she says
in her Israeli accent,
you, Louise – you are so –
exciting!

My teacher
who gathers around her
the brightest and the best,
she invited me to dinner
and others of us, together,
to tea
and to walk

For This

Why did I step off the edge of the cliff
at the new millennium,
for what?

I didn't know how I would survive,
only that I would

Only that somehow,
stepping into the unknown,
my heart would keep beating,
would start breathing

> Why did you survive
> when no one said that you could,
> when you stepped off that cliff of your own
> ten years before?

For me, it was for the last vertebra
to be put into motion;
for the finding of oneness
between the two sides of my face;
it was to be washed through;
it was for the holding and the fears and compulsions
to be filtered, siphoned,
so that the sunshine of smiling
could shine through

It was for this, for this –
for both of us, it was for this –
or something like it

Directions Home

1.

Sitting side by side on the couch we converse
this is what's happened, and this
my friend has come back from Africa
though she will be gone again
and she wants to know, really wants to know –
what will you do now
and what do you think will happen, she says

2.

Conversation moves diagonally across the table
and laterally side by side
as I eat with my North Carolina cousins, conversing
of Sub-Saharan Africans and Episcopal churches and priests
Over breakfast they feed back to me
how and why my work is important,
these cousins who really care

3.

Standing on top of the third bald mountain
past the maintained part of the trail
finding the trail now with feet only,
blueberry thickets sometimes over our heads
We halt at the end, at the last outcropping,
witness the quiet, the stillness, the breath,
and we come to know a friend

4.

In lawnchairs we laugh in my neighbor's front yard,
swapping tales of fury and love
we laugh till we cry at the outrage
of directions given sloppy, and wrong

* * * * *

My Portugese ex-roommate
and my Russian roommate, both
complain that in America everyone is so polite
that everything stays on the surface here
that they never know what anyone
really means

I know this to be true and that
with no families
to laugh and scream and cry with,
this helps keep us
so alone

Criss-crossing the continent over and over,
seeking loved ones, my children, friends,
I find these windows of connection, proving
that I am not crazy, I know what I need –
these directions home, my friend

About the Author

Louise Morgan Runyon holds a B.A. in English and Theatre Arts from Oberlin College, and is a modern dancer/choreographer as well as poet. She is Artistic Director of Louise Runyon Performance Company which has presented dance, poetry and puppetry at Atlanta venues since 1989. She has toured her one-woman show, *Crones, Dolls and Raging Beauties,* throughout the Southeast and the nation, and has performed her poetry at the Southern Women Writers Conference in Rome, Georgia; in New Mexico, New York, Oregon, Kentucky and North Carolina; and in Atlanta at venues including the Decatur Book Festival, the High Museum, Callanwolde Fine Arts Center, Emory University, Seven Stages, the Decatur Arts Festival, DeKalb County Public Library, Java Monkey Speaks, Barnes & Noble, Very Special Arts Georgia, Portfolio Center and the Arts Festival of Atlanta. She published her first book of poems, *Reborn*, in 2004, and her work has appeared in *Java Monkey Speaks*, *Volumes I and II*, and in *Golden Poetry: A Celebration of Southern Poets 50 and Older, Volume II*. Runyon is a practitioner of the FELDENKRAIS METHOD® of somatic education (somatic = the lived experience of mind and body together as one).

Front Cover Painting: John T. Morgan
Front Cover Photography: Dan Schultz
Back Cover Photography: Lucas Barth (www.LucasBarth.com)
Cover Design: Lucas Barth

To contact Louise Morgan Runyon
about poetry performances:

Louise Morgan Runyon
P.O. Box 33601
Decatur, Georgia 30033-33601
LouiseRunyon130@bellsouth.net

To order this book, or for information
about upcoming performances:

www.LouiseRunyon.blogspot.com
LouiseRunyon@aol.com